William Lloyd

Saints of 1881

Sketches of lives of St. Clare of Montefalco, St. Laurence of Brindisi, St. Benedict Joseph Labre, St. John Baptist de Rossi

William Lloyd

Saints of 1881

Sketches of lives of St. Clare of Montefalco, St. Laurence of Brindisi, St. Benedict Joseph Labre, St. John Baptist de Rossi

ISBN/EAN: 9783741178054

Manufactured in Europe, USA, Canada, Australia, Japa

Cover: Foto ©Andreas Hilbeck / pixelio.de

Manufactured and distributed by brebook publishing software (www.brebook.com)

William Lloyd

Saints of 1881

SAINTS OF 1881

OR

SKETCHES OF LIVES OF

ST. CLARE OF MONTEFALCO.
ST. LAURENCE OF BRINDISI.
ST. BENEDICT JOSEPH LABRE.
ST. JOHN BAPTIST DE ROSSI

BY
WILLIAM LLOYD
PRIEST OF THE DIOCESE OF WESTMINSTER

LONDON: BURNS & OATES.
1882

ADVERTISEMENT.

The following Sketches, undertaken at the Publishers' request, have been put together hastily, and under the pressure of much other work.

I am under great obligations to the Fathers of the London Oratory. With a courtesy and generosity which I shall not forget, their magnificent library was put at my service, and everything done that could make my work easier. Two of the saints, sketched in this little volume, may well encourage the faithful in devotion to St. Philip.

Occurring in our own times, the Canonizations are meant to teach lessons to ourselves. I cannot hope that these hasty pages will do much in bringing those lessons home to us; but, till fuller lives are written, they may supply a want, and rekindle here and there love of holiness of life and trust in His grace who is wonderful in His saints.

ISLEWORTH,
December, 1881.

ST. CLARE OF MONTEFALCO.

Some ten or twelve miles north of Spoleto, on the road to Foligno, stands the little town of Montefalco. That beautiful hill-country of Umbria may well be, as it is, the home of Saints. Siena, Perugia, Orvieto, Viterbo, Asisi —no one that has seen them will forget them. Their names have become symbols of all that is most beautiful in the world of nature and art and grace.

At Montefalco, our saint was born. It was about the year 1275—twenty-two years after her name-saint died at Asisi. The name of our Saint's father was Damian, and we may notice that the ruined convent at Asisi, which St. Francis rebuilt, was the convent of St. Damian—it was there he led St. Clare and her sister, Agnes, then a child of fourteen. There the Order of Poor Clares was founded; there she was visited in her last illness by Innocent IV. and his Cardinals; there she died; nor ever left it till they carried her out for burial to the convent of St. George, which stood within the walls. The famous church, too, at Anagni was the church of St. Damian.

Damian, and his wife, Jacqueline, deserved the blessing of saintly children. Their own lives were exemplary; giving no offence to any man, and walking in all the commandments of the Lord without blame. They had a daughter Jane, older than our Saint; and certainly if we needed to describe how far the spirit of those old centuries differed from our own, no better illustration could be chosen than that which is furnished by Damian's little household. In mere childhood, Jane had withdrawn, with her parents' consent, to a spot known as St. Leonard's. There she had gathered about her a number of other maidens of her own age and spirit; and there, without attaching themselves to any order, they were living the life hidden with God. Almost from babyhood Clara longed to join her sister's community.

St. Clare of Montefalco.

She made it the subject of especial prayer; she prepared herself for the grace, on which she had set her heart, by austerities from which robust men would have shrunk; till at last, at the age of six, her importunities and tears prevailed, and the child was received. Truly, God is wonderful in His saints.

Her act of thanksgiving was an eight days' fast, taking nothing each day beyond an apple and a little bread. And as she began she continued. Her common daily fare was a very small loaf with a draught of water; for days together she would forego even this scanty food. On Sundays, and the more solemn feasts, she added a few wild herbs or dried beans, which she would steep in water. Her bed was a plank on the bare ground: she wore none but the roughest garments, sometimes a hair shirt, and often disciplined herself to blood. They knew in those days what it was to carry about the mortification or death of Jesus Crucified in their bodies.

We are reminded of the Baptist's desert

life, with its scanty meat and raiment, and its union with God, as we read the accounts of Clara's childhood. Vision after vision was vouchsafed her in the narrow oratory which her sister had set apart for her use.

St. Leonard's was becoming inconveniently small, and Jane, Superior still of the growing community, decided to remove to the summit of St. Catherine's Hill, at no great distance from St. Leonard's. They had seen one day a cross of light shining over the hill, and followed by a procession of prayerful women; and they had felt that the vision was as the finger of God marking out their new home. They went, and on that lonely summit built their humble monastery, but not till contradictions and obstacles, betraying almost incredible malice, had been met and overcome. But they were not to be daunted, Clare's unflagging resoluteness throughout the proceedings being conspicuous even where all were brave and resolute.

At their request the Bishop of Spoleto, in whose diocese they were, gave them a rule—

the rule of St. Augustine. The expenses of building, however, had exhausted their slender resources, and it was plain that if they could hope to live at all it must be as mendicants. Clare a mendicant! There was perhaps no aspect of the spiritual life from which she would have turned with so much dread; but then if *she* did not beg, another must. That was argument enough for her, and she volunteered for the work. She toiled from house to house on her weary errand, but she could never be induced to set foot beyond the threshold. There would have been the distraction of seeing and being seen, and the danger to her rule of silence. So when the mountain rain was falling pitilessly, she stood outside, accepting only such shelter as the street afforded, and when an alms was given she received it kneeling, in sign of her gratitude to the Giver, first, of all good gifts and next to her benefactor. All this while she neither interrupted nor relaxed the severity of her fasting and other mortifications. She was rapidly wearing out her life;

and at last the community saw that the one chance of her being spared to them depended on their withdrawing her forthwith from the out-door work, which had edified the neighbourhood no less than the community.

Returning to her seclusion she flung herself with redoubled delight into her life of prayer, silence, and manifold penance. One day, when she had spoken without sufficiently grave necessity, she punished herself by baring her feet and standing barefooted in ice-cold water, repeating meantime devoutly, and without haste, a hundred *Our Fathers*. As self-punishment for failing in our holy purposes is unflinching, so will our progress in the ways of holiness be certain as well as rapid. She avoided as carefully as she could the parlour, where visitors were entertained. When it could not be avoided she still carried with her the love of silence and seclusion, which was the secret of her close union with God. She would keep her face strictly veiled—seldom raising her voice above the lowest tone, or answering beyond a monosyllable. Once, when she had come from her brother, after an interview during which she had in no particular relaxed her rule, and her sister had suggested that for her own brother at all events she might remove her veil, she pleaded that as we spoke with the tongue, not with the eyes, we might be satisfied with hearing the voice without seeing the face. She was chosen by her Spouse for the contemplative life. Had she wished to multiply occasions of holding converse with her relatives, she might have served God in the bosom of her peaceful and holy home. She had gone out into solitude to be more alone with Him who was henceforth to be to her father and brother, and home, and all things; nor did she care to leave Him needlessly even for those who by natural ties were most near and dear to her. In the days of his silent life the Baptist would have had scant dealings with his parents, for all their sanctity, had they sought to break in on his solitude.

There was not a menial work to be done but Clare was foremost in doing it—not a nun over-burdened with her office, but Clare noticed it and was full of helpfulness. Her sister fell ill; our saint's prayers restored her. It was not to be for long, however. She had borne the heats of the day and the burdens. The evening was at hand, with the rest that remaineth to the people of God, and the reward that is promised to the good and faithful servant. She had been Superior of Holy Cross, the convent on St. Catherine's Hill, some eight years when she died; and Clare, to whom was revealed her sister's enjoyment of the Beatific Vision, was chosen Abbess in her sister's place.

She struggled hard against it, but without avail. Her new dignity must not dispense her from any fragment of her rule. On the contrary, it must be a new motive for exactitude and cheerful obedience. So she understood it, and her exemplary life became a living rule, encouraging and correcting all, and making perseverance less difficult. She was not careless of their bodily needs for fear that such anxieties might interfere with their spirit of prayer, and make the spiritual life insupportably disheartening. We are told how once, when Montefalco and the villages about St. Catherine's were wasted by famine, and her nuns were absolutely without bread, He who fed His people in the desert with manna fashioned by the hands of angels, now sent His angels in visible shape to minister to His chosen servants. In their hands those ministering angels bore baskets laden with bread, that, like the widow's vessel of meal, wasted not till the day when the famine had passed from the land.

Her antipathy to the parlour still lasted, to the extreme discomfiture of the ladies round about—"those great talkers who are always bringing the world into the cloister." Poverty, the constant recollection of God's majesty, in whose sight we always stand, devotion to the Passion of Our Lord, systematic and bountiful almsgiving, were among the holy practices she laboured hardest to develop in her nuns. Whenever they baked for the community, twelve of the finest loaves were set aside, in honour of the twelve apostles, to be given to the poor. Of her own meals nearly everything was reserved for them. Her charity likewise for the most needy and helpless of all Christ's poor—the Faithful Departed not yet resting in peace—was most keen and practical; and not a day passed but the Office of the Dead was recited in choir after the canonical hours. The sick who came to the abbey-gates were sure of a welcome, and tender treatment. A poor, ulcerous creature appeared one day so loathsome a mass of disease, that, for the moment, her strong heart quailed, and she was on the point of fainting. Another moment and she had recollected herself, and fixing her eyes steadily upon the sore, she bent over and kissed it reverently, and sucked out the virulent matter. She must discipline herself out of the natural repugnance which all men feel for the Lazarus who is lying at our gates.

Her humility was sorely tried by the deference and respect shown to her as Superior. There was no escape possible from the place of honour in choir and chapter and refectory; everywhere else, in the scullery, in the sick-room, and about the house, she was free to make herself as the servant of the lowest—gladly assisting even the youngest of the novices.

The purity of an angel will help us to form an idea of the purity of her whom indeed God had made little less than the angels. She had once, at the age of eleven, been rebuked by her sister for a slight, indeed involuntary, carelessness. She did penance for it as though the little thoughtlessness, if it were even so much, had been an enormous sin. In the matter of purity, the saints have their standard; the world has its standard, and there is increasing danger that Christian men and women will be found at last to have been satisfied with ordering their lives in this matter by the world's standard—not the saints'.

We need not dwell on her love for Jesus in His Holy Sacrament. Her whole life was a spiritual communion; and on two occasions He blessed for her, as He has blessed for others among His saints, her yearning for the Bread of Life by giving her with His own hand the Mystery of His Body and Blood. What He had done for His apostles, He has done since, when His saints by their transcendent devotion to His sacramental presence have merited the grace.

In keeping with all the rest was her devotion to His sacred Passion. It was in her thoughts night and day; always on her lips in her instructions to the nuns. She had made it a special prayer that she might be granted to see in spirit all that He had suffered on Calvary and the road that led to Calvary. And her prayer had been granted. Her wish to realize what He had undergone for her was fulfilled. In her brows she felt agonies of torture as vivid as though the thorns were piercing through to the brain. The taste of vinegar and gall was in her mouth; her hands and feet quivered as though the nails were tearing through flesh and sinews; her body was tortured as though men had scourged it till they were weary of scourging. The shrinking from death, the bitter agony of heart that could find no outlet but in the sweat of blood, the shame and pain of nakedness,—all these things were imprinted on her very soul and life with so much mysterious reality that she became a living image of Jesus the Crucified. Even beyond many saints it was vouchsafed to her to carry about the death of Jesus Crucified in her body.

No wonder she spoke of His Passion as few probably have spoken. But so long as we are in the flesh, even our graces are not without their danger. We must watch always as well as pray always. Clare was one day, in a conference with her nuns, dwelling on her favourite theme. A nun interrupted with the remark that she had never been visited with the consolations and the power of realizing our Lord's sufferings, which the Abbess had promised to those who would meditate assiduously on the Passion. The remark aroused in Clare's mind a momentary feeling, we are not told whether of impatience or vanity. She could not be said to have consented, and yet she did not repel it as promptly and generously as her Lord had a right to expect. And certainly the awfulness of venial sin—the least and least deliberate—could not well be more fitly illustrated than by the punishment her fault, slight seemingly, and hardly perceptible, needed to undergo before reparation had been duly made to the sanctity and justice of God. It was a terrible chastisement. For eleven years He withdrew Himself from her. Eleven years of appalling spiritual desolation, scruples, weariness, temptations, bodily sickness, to atone for a moment's failure to correspond generously with His grace—it shows, if anything was needed to show, what sin is and what the sanctity of God is. With an energy beyond her wont, she fasted, wore hair shirts, scourged herself to blood with constant disciplines, wept and prayed, but unavailingly. It was a road she needs must travel. No more visions and revelations for her, and colloquies with her One Beloved; no more delight in God's service, nor sweetness in prayer, nor the exquisite joy of knowing that she was in deed and in

St. Clare of Montefalco.

truth in His grace; only movements of blasphemy henceforward, and imaginations as unclean and frightful as hell could suggest. Awful as it was, it was her Purgatory—the fire which burnt away the dross and left the silver seven times refined. And awful as it was, she never flinched throughout; those unnamable imaginings never wrung from her even a half-consent to pleasure, or doubt or despair, or so much as a passing thought of bitterness or distrust in Him who was leading her whither He would along paths of His own choosing. She was never weary of begging prayers of pious souls that in His own time His just anger against her might be appeased.

At last, but not till eleven years had gone, the tempest was stilled, and there arose a great calm. Was the light less welcome after such a night of utter darkness? The trial had been extreme, but He, who with temptation will make a way to escape, had brought her safely through, and her reward was at hand. From this time nothing was to separate her from her love of God which is in Christ Jesus our Lord.

Her revelations were renewed; and a multitude of extraordinary favours—visions, ecstasies, miracles—granted to her which fill a whole book in the process of her canonization. She told in prophecy how Cardinal Colonna would be deposed from his Cardinalate and later reinstated. Both events were fulfilled; and on his restoration the Cardinal sent a treasure priceless in value to her—a relic of St. Anne. She announced to her Ordinary, the Bishop of Spoleto, that he would be raised to a still higher office. He became Cardinal and Bishop of Ostia. As years earlier she had been privileged to behold in a vision the scenes of the Passion, so one Christmas night she was rapt into ecstasy and beheld, in all its lowliness and all its glory, the birth of her eternal King and Spouse, even Christ the Lord, in the city of David. For days and months together she lived entirely without food. Of a truth, the saints may well say: Not by bread alone doth man live. One ecstasy of which we read lasted without interruption from the Epiphany till the Purification, twenty-seven days, during which time, as she gazed on her Lord seated on His throne of majesty at His Father's right hand, she saw great multitudes of souls winging their way upwards to their rest in His presence. Few, very few, she has told us so entered into the joy of their Lord till the earthliness and defilement that still clung to them at the hour of death had been burnt away in the purifying fire of purgatory. "I have been looking," He said to her at this time, "for a spot where I can plant my cross. Thy heart is a fitting place; suffer it to take root there." He speaks likewise to all His creatures, though for us His words may not have the same abundance of meaning, nor find their fulfilment in the same visible way, as in the case of St. Clare. We read of the secrets of consciences manifested to her, of her speaking with the gift of tongues, of an infused knowledge of the mysteries of the faith, which gave her power to confute and put to shame those who dared to make an attempt to entangle her in the specious arguments of heresies then prevalent.

Her life was a light that could not be hid. From far and near they flocked, if only to see Clare of Montefalco; if possible, to ask her prayers.˙ Their sick and dying, and in some cases their dead, were brought to her; and at her touch or prayers they were healed.

It is not easy to ascertain how long this period of her life must have lasted, but the end was approaching. She had lived for Him alone, and close as had been her union with Him here, she was going to see Him face to face. As the hart panted after the fountains of water, her soul panted after Him. "Oh, when shall I come and appear before the face of God?" He had told her years beforehand when the end would come; and now as the August came round of 1308 she knew that the month had dawned of which, on this earth, she would not see the end. It was the month in which St. Clare of Asisi had died, fifty-one years ago. No Pope or Cardinals gathered about the death-bed of St. Clare of Montefalco, but He whom her soul loved came to her, and His angels came with Him. He told her

St. Clare of Montefalco.

that her journey was finishing; told her that her eleven years of fiery anguish had preserved many from an evil death and judgment; told her that no slightest stain was left which she had not washed out by her years of penance. Little wonder that as those early August days slipped by, she seemed rather in heaven than on earth. Her last Communion—if her biographers had had the tongue of angels—*that* would have been beyond their describing. Then they anointed her, and eternity, she felt, was very close. "You will find," she told her children, "the cross of Jesus graven on my heart." She saw through the opened heavens the glory that had been prepared for her, and, bewildered and wondering, protested aloud that His reward for her little work was too great—too great.

The eleventh came, the day of her name-saint's death; the twelfth, the day of her burial; the Assumption came, enkindling her love and yearning—but she had not gone. Two days later—or was it the 18th? the authorities differ—and the good fight was fought and won; the uncaged bird had flown upwards into the light. *Volabo, ut passer.* "I will fly as a sparrow; like one of small weight and little skill, I will flutter into the bosom of my God!"

They were to find the cross of Jesus graven on her heart. In hands and feet and side, the wounds made by lance and nails were imprinted on St. Francis of Asisi, as the fruit of his constant meditation on the Passion, and the reward of his bodily penance. And when he died, not fifty years before our saint was born, the faithful were free to look upon the wounds; and on that Sunday morning, when they bore his sacred body from the Portiuncula, and the procession on its way to the church of St. George, halted at St. Damian's, St. Clare, in her holy eagerness, attempted to draw out one of the nails that protruded above the wound. The nail could not be dislodged. Only a little fresh blood oozed out, which she gathered on a linen cloth and treasured reverently.

When our saint died, they divided her heart, and on the two surfaces so laid open, they found, formed by veinlet and tissue, the image of Jesus Crucified and the emblems of His Passion. When Moses came from his interview with God, God's glory shone about the face of His servant. Is there anything improbable or exceptionally wonderful, when we remember God's dealings with His saints, that the servant who, throughout her life, had been face to face with the Passion of Jesus Crucified, should bear away upon her heart the sign of His plentiful redemption? He who could make the unborn infant bear witness to the Incarnation, could also make heart, or face, or hands of His servants bear witness to His glory or His Passion. Many saints besides St. Francis, St. Philip Neri, and St. Veronica Giuliani, will occur, as instances more or less analogous, to those familiar with the lives of saints.

The doubts of the Vicar-General of the diocese may serve to set our doubts at rest. He came from the Bishop, convinced that it was all mere women's fancy, and in spite of the evidence before his eyes, he angrily dashed a knife or razor through one of the two parts by way of making short work of such delusions! His consternation gave place to an act of faith as, on the two fresh surfaces now disclosed, he saw no less distinctly the figure of his crucified Master and the instruments of His suffering.

Eight years after her death, John XXII., in two bulls, ordered the process of her canonization, but it was interrupted at his death. Three hundred years afterwards Urban VIII. (1623-1644) published the bull of her beatification. In our own days, nearly six centuries after her death, she is to be crowned with the aureola of Saint. Why should the Church have had to wait so long for her latest triumph? We know not. But neither do we know why the world had to wait wearily through thousands of years for the coming of the Prince of Peace.

To such a century as our own the silent life of Clare on her Umbrian hill will be a puzzle or a mistake. It ought to be a reminder that one thing is necessary—to live

St. Clare of Montefalco. 23

for God, and to keep oneself unspotted from the world, if we would be safe in the life everlasting.

WE FOOLS ESTEEMED THEIR LIFE MADNESS, AND THEIR END WITHOUT HONOUR. BEHOLD HOW THEY ARE NUMBERED AMONG THE CHILDREN OF GOD, AND THEIR LOT IS AMONG THE SAINTS.

ST. LAURENCE OF BRINDISI.

WE turn to a very different life—a type of the active, as the last was a type of the contemplative, life. It represents strikingly the eternal conflict between the Church and the world, and of it may be said what has justly been said of the life of St. Bernard, that to write it thoroughly would require the history of many nations during the years in which he lived. When Father Laurence died, the Duke of Bavaria, foremost of the Catholic champions of his time, declared that he had lost the best adviser, wisest director, and truest friend he had ever known. A higher tribute is that of his biographer, who considers that Blessed Laurence was not merely among the greatest men of his own time, but among the greatest that history has ever had to deal with.

St. Laurence of Brindisi. 25

The year of his birth was 1559. It was an eventful time. In the August of that year Paul IV. died, and was succeeded in December by Pius IV. Mary had succeeded to the throne of England in the year preceding, St. Francis Xavier has been dead these six years; St. Ignatius three; Luther not more than thirteen—events which need no commentary to manifest their importance. St. Philip Neri was still in Rome; ordained these eight years. St. Charles was in Milan, not yet a priest. Within three years from this date the sessions of the Council of Trent, after a ten-years' interruption, will be resumed.

The day of his birth, July 22nd, is noticeable, as on that same day, sixty years later, he breathed his last. His father, William de' Rossi, was living at Brindisi, no longer the busy seaport of classical times—indeed, little more than a village in the midst of olive woods. His parents, as though from a presentiment that a great career was before him, gave him in baptism the name of Julius Cæsar; and when in very early childhood he showed a leaning towards monastic life, their piety encouraged him. They placed him in the Franciscan Convent at Brindisi.

They both died when he was very young. On their death he went to Venice, then in possession of all the coast-lands of the Adriatic and Ægean. It was not, however, the political importance of Venice that invited Laurence to his new home on the Adriatic. The Superior of the flourishing College of St. Mark, at Venice, was his uncle—a man of considerable learning, and naturally interested in his orphan nephew.

On the 18th of February, 1575—it was the year of the Jubilee in Rome, and Laurence was not quite sixteen—he joined the Capuchins at Verona. The reformed branch of the Franciscan Order, named Capuchins from their hoods, had been begun in Tuscany exactly fifty years before this date, and three years later, in 1528, approved by Clement VII. Still, in its first fervour, the Capuchin branch had an attraction which he could not resist, for the boy, whose earliest memories were bound up with the great family of St. Francis. His high-sounding baptismal name, Julius Cæsar, he laid aside, never to be resumed, for the humbler and more Christian name of Brother Laurence. The neighbouring University of Padua, though it never rivalled the fame of Paris, was yet deservedly renowned as a centre of great learning and intellectual activity. Laurence was gifted with conspicuous abilities; and his strong and innocent character gave promise that he would be proof against the corrupt life and disbelief for which Padua was too notorious, in spite of its learning. Its evil name, as a hotbed of rationalism, had been strengthened by the publication there of the *De Immortalitate* of Pomponatius, the most celebrated Aristotelian of his age, and successor in the chair of philosophy at Padua, to Ficinus, the no less distinguished Platonist. The sunlight falls on filth and pestilence, and is not defiled; and Laurence lived and breathed in the infected air of Padua, but neither his purity nor his faith was tarnished.

In addition to Latin and Greek, for which Padua gave him the highest possible facilities, he studied Hebrew — a subject rarer then than now; and worked at it so diligently that he became a finished Hebrew scholar. Not so long before this, when the Complutensian Polyglott was published (1522), the preface contained a remark that they print the Vulgate column between the Hebrew and the Greek, like Christ between two thieves! Since then the study of Greek had spread widely, but the perfect mastery of Hebrew was uncommon— so uncommon that the reputation of our Saint's Hebrew attainments had travelled far beyond the limits of the University, and when, at the end of a brilliant scholastic career, he was ordained to the priesthood in spite of his humility, and gaining a great harvest of souls by the unction of his preaching, Clement VIII. called him to Rome to labour for the conversion of the Jews. The wisdom of the Pope's choice was proved by the results, the blessing which had accompanied his first labours in the ministry following him still. His knowledge of the Hebrew text of the sacred books was a veritable power to him in his work, and he wielded it with extraordinary effect. Conversions began in unexpected numbers, and continued to increase. It was an unusual harvest even for the zeal of Saints, and the name of Blessed Laurence became a household word throughout Italy. His praise was throughout all the Churches, till there was no withstanding longer their petitions that they might be privileged to listen to his holy eloquence, and profit by his holy life and enlightened counsel. He began a missionary journey which embraced nearly every city of importance throughout Italy. Everywhere the fruit was the same—reverent admiration of his transcendent gifts, and of the light which could not be hid of his unmistakable union with God; and the higher fruit of the conversion of souls, without which all the tribute of admiration and applause is meaningless, or hypocrisy and insult. *Qui non ardet non incendit;* and conversely, he who is himself on fire will be likely to enkindle with his own fire those with whom he comes in contact. Such gifts as his, developed by such years of preparation and constant progress in the life of prayer, could not fail of extraordinary results when seed-time had given place to the harvest. Nor were the results less marvellous when from his missionary toils he was recalled and appointed as Professor in the Chair of Theology.

Theology, as he understood it, was a thing of the heart, as well as of the mind. Exact scientific investigation of theological truth was in no danger in his hands of being dry and lifeless. As it poured from his burning heart all fused and molten, it filled the souls of his students with love as well as knowledge, and many of them lived to bear tribute to the character of his teaching by the high rank they held among the preachers and theologians of their day. His system was adopted later by Thomassinus of the Oratory, and Petavius the Jesuit.

That was at Venice, where he was in

charge of the convent of the Holy Redeemer, known as the "Della Zueca." Michael of Bologna, the saintly lay-brother whom he commissioned here to remind him unsparingly of his faults, and whom we find as our Saint's companion in his subsequent journeys as Provincial, must have found his post a sinecure. Occasionally, he might have to remind Father Laurence that it was time to finish study, or prayer, or other duty, and that was all.

His name had become famous for administrative talent in consequence of the conspicuous skill and tact with which he had fulfilled the difficult post of the "Della Zueca," and afterwards of Superior of the house at Bassano. Suddenly—it seemed so complete and unexpected a departure from their usual procedure—at a Chapter held at Cortona, Jan. 16, 1590, they chose the young Bassano Superior—then barely thirty years of age—Provincial of Tuscany, cradle and home of the family of St. Francis. With might and main he fought against the dignity so thrust upon him—but the Cortona election was ratified by a peremptory command from the General, and he had no alternative but to submit.

Three years later, 1593, Venice elected him Provincial, and won him back. He had begun his provincial visitation in a remote corner of the province when news reached him that his uncle was dying—good old Peter de' Rossi, at whose school Laurence, the little orphan fresh from home, had been bound to lay aside his Franciscan habit for the cassock of the secular priesthood. That had not been done without a pang, but in spite of his boyish distress he had spent several happy years with his uncle, and had never forgotten the heavy debt due to him as his second father.

And now, when obstacles were many, and it seemed impossible to reach Venice in time, nothing could hold him back. In an incredibly—miraculously, some of his biographers have thought—short time he was back in Venice, ministering at the good old uncle's deathbed. Surely the aged man must have

St. Laurence of Brindisi. 33

felt that his spending and being spent for such a nephew had not been in vain.

There Laurence remained, soothing, encouraging, praying, as though outside that sick-room he had no single work or care till he had closed the old man's eyes in death. Then Laurence followed him to the grave and resumed his visitation.

An important event in the Order was at hand. At the old Convent of St. Bonaventure, under the Quirinal in Rome, they assembled for their twenty-second General Chapter. It was the last day of May, 1596. St. Philip died the May before, not half-an-hour's walk distant. At this Chapter Laurence was named Definitor General.

It was arranged that he should make a visitation of their houses throughout Sicily, when a letter written to Clement VIII. by Rodolf II., Emperor of Germany, and Berka, Archbishop of Prague, gave an altogether new direction to his life. The Emperor, alarmed at the ravages the Reformers had made throughout Germany, petitioned the Holy

Father for a body of Capuchins, to found houses in the districts of his kingdom which seemed immediately threatened. They were to serve, as the letter expressed it, as a sort of outlying fortification; they were to bear the first assaults of the enemy, and to keep the foe altogether at a distance from the citadel. Of the little army chosen for this unequal campaign, "Father Brindisi" was the leader. His forces consisted of eleven priests and two lay-brothers; but if God is with us, who shall be against us? He bore down every opposition, and within a year of entering on his new work, had founded houses of the Order in Vienna, Prague, and in Gratz, the principal city of Styria.*

His work in the German Empire did not end with the founding of his houses. The Emperor Rodolf, his mind as yet uninfluenced by Court intrigue, had come to recognise the noble character and splendid talents hidden under that coarse Franciscan habit. He had

---

* In the order given here, not, as Rohrbacher states, first at Prague and next at Vienna.

a commission to give where much would depend on the choice he made of his ambassador. The Turks, thirsting to wipe out their defeat at Lepanto (1571), were advancing along the Danube, and had announced their resolve of taking possession of Hungary. Mahomet III. was at their head. Germany, rent by feuds and civil war, consequent on the Reformation, seemed unconscious of its danger, and single-handed Rodolf could not hope to prove a match for the Ottoman hosts as numberless, seemingly, as an invasion of locusts. Who should be sent to rally the laggards round the imperial standard—to make them feel, Catholic and Protestant alike, that they were only one remove from destruction, when Rodolf was overpowered—and to fill them with courage and the assurance of victory? It was a singular mission for the Capuchin monk; but at Protestant Courts and Catholic his success was complete, and the answer to his appeal so universal and immediate, that, by 1598, the combined armies were formed, and put under the command of

Matthias, the Emperor's brother, as generalissimo.

The years slipped by as the struggle continued, with nothing especially memorable on either side, when, as if to show that the army which the Capuchin monk had got together could not be kept together without him, the Commander-in-chief obtained from the Pope an order that Laurence should join the army forthwith, and devote himself to the one work of preparing the soldiers by prayer and penance for the victory which he had never ceased to promise them.

The October of 1601 came—that same month, thirty years ago exactly, the Turks had their pride broken at Lepanto. Now they had crossed the Danube, and in numbers, variously estimated between 80,000 and 90,000, they were drawn up a few miles from Albareale. Laurence, on horseback, in his Capuchin habit and cross in hand, had been haranguing the Christian army, drawn up before him in line of battle. They were less than thirty thousand strong. His burning words went home, to such effect that the soldiers could scarcely be induced to wait for the command to charge. His promise of victory was explicit. Meantime, in a council of war, some of the imperial officers were urging violently the madness of risking an engagement. The enemy had all the high ground, and outnumbered them almost as three to one. They must beat a retreat as best they could. Matthias was perplexed. What was he to do? F. Laurence had better be sent for—part of his commission, in the brief appointing him, was to give advice when advice was needed.

Laurence came into the council, his heart still burning with the words from which he had been preaching to the soldiers, " Fear ye not, and be not dismayed. To-morrow you shall go out against them, and the Lord will be with you " (2 Paral. xx. 17.) He made short work of the waverers; and, indeed, there was something about his certainty of victory different from mere human certainty, and making their halting policy look foolish and out of place. They decided to give battle.

On the day of battle a monk was again or

horseback, cross in hand, in advance of the front rank. No need to say the monk was Father Laurence. He speaks a few words that he knows so well how to drive straight home to a soldier's heart, and with a fury that baffles all description they charge upon the infidel. The Turks were not so easily broken, and for hours the battle raged fast and furiously, till at last a final charge from the Christian side broke up the Turkish ranks, and they fled in extreme confusion. The Christian forces got possession of the rising ground—seized all their large artillery, and by evening had gained a decisive victory. That was October 11th, 1601.

Decisive as the battle was, Mahomet III. would not recognise as yet that he had been hopelessly defeated. Three days afterwards he hazarded another battle. It was on this occasion (not on the 11th as Rohrbacher represents) that our Saint in a moment of reverie or prayer, was hurried by his horse into the thick of the fray, and before he had time to collect himself, he was surrounded by the enemy. Two colonels, Rosbourg and Altain, rescued him. This was no place for him, they reminded him, and begged him to go to the rear. "This is my place," was his answer, "and here I will stay. Soldiers, another charge." Quick as lightning they charged, and, before long, panic had seized the Turks, and another Christian victory had been won. When Mahomet recrossed the Danube, he had lost thirty thousand of his finest soldiers—" Next to God and Our Lady," said De Mercurio, second in command to Matthias, "we owe that victory to Father Laurence." And on the day of his beatification (1783) the scene painted over the great door of St. Peter's, was the battle of Albareale. Underneath ran the legend, "When Austria was in sorest straits, Blessed Laurence of Brindisi, Cross in hand, struck terror into the enemies of Christ and put them to flight." One soldier who had witnessed his wonderful power, and no less wonderful escapes, begged to be admitted among his monks as a lay-brother, and as Brother Francis of Gorizia,* crowned an edifying life by a saintly death. It is worth noticing, too, that of the many heretical soldiers, who before the battle of the eleventh had made no attempt to conceal their contempt for the soldier-monk, not one was contemptuous or disrespectful when he appeared at their head on the day of the fourteenth. Indeed, many fell on their knees and with the faith and humility of Catholic soldiers begged for a special benediction.

However, with the retreat of Mahomet his work, as soldier-priest, was at an end, and he made at once for Italy. A great part of his journey he did on foot, and throughout, he kept his name a strict secret for fear of the enthusiasm his presence would certainly awaken were he once recognised. It was the year of the General Chapter (1602) and he would satisfy his longing to give outward expression to his child-like love for the Blessed Virgin by a visit to Loreto. At Loreto,

* Or Görz, in the Isonzothal, some thirty-five miles from Trieste.

St. Laurence of Brindisi. 41

accordingly, he spent the Lent, serving all the Masses that were said in the Holy House humbly, as though he were still the little Brindisi boy in his Franciscan habit.

At Easter, he went on to Rome, his heart yearning as he trudged along the hilly road, that at last might be given him a few years of rest to devote himself in the quiet of his cell to union with God and the sanctification of his own soul. In consideration of his gout and other maladies the Holy Father had authorized him to make his journeys on horseback, or in a litter, but exemptions were not after the heart of Father Brindisi, and he preferred to walk, taking as his whole retinue one lay-brother.

He assisted at the General Chapter, and gave his account of the foundation of their new houses in Bohemia and Austria. What was his dismay when, as the election of the General came on, every vote fell on the young priest who had come among them fresh from founding three new provinces and leading the Christian hosts to victory! It was then—it may be still—a unique position for a monk not forty-three years of age to find himself duly elected General of the Capuchins.

The General's first work was his visitation. It was his inspection of the troops. It was the father's seeing for himself that every member of his household was abiding by its rules, and cared for with fatherly kindness. He went by Milan to Switzerland, then through Flanders into France, and afterwards into Spain. From Spain he made his way back to Germany. He returned to Italy, and had got as far as Naples, when the news reached him of the death of Clement VIII. (1605). His term of office, as General, ended this year; but as if to make it clear that for him there would be no rest on this side of the grave, at the conclusion of his generalship he was sent off hurriedly to Germany to try to stem the tide of persecution that had arisen against the new Order. He knew not what fear meant. Where the whole populace was " breathing out threatenings and slaughter," Laurence would mount the pulpit and denounce and reprove, and persuade with utter fearlessness. The common stratagem of appealing to Hebrew texts, as bearing out this or the other point of "Reformed" doctrine, was too transparent to be attempted upon him.

He was in Germany when the dissensions, consequent on the vexed question of the Dukedom of Cleves, were at their height. John William, the last duke, was dead, and numerous pretenders sprang up at once to the vacant dukedom. It became a religious war, and was the origin of the famous Protestant League. The League had gone through many vicissitudes, but at this moment was strengthened by the adherence of Henry IV. of France. The Catholic princes of Germany, making common cause in self-defence, had formed themselves into a Catholic League under the leadership of Maximilian, Duke of Bavaria. The Duke had been most staunch in his feelings of friendship and reverence for our Saint, since his visit to Munich, the Bavarian capital, in 1599. On that occasion

Laurence had brought healing and peace to Maximilian's household by freeing his wife from the evil spirit that possessed her, and by promising him a son who should inherit the dukedom. Since those days a son had been born, and Maximilian's veneration for Father da Brindisi was almost unbounded.

To the keen sight of F. Laurence it was plain, during this visit of 1605, that unless the Catholic League could form a most powerful allliance to counterbalance the adherence of Henry IV. to the other side, the Catholic League might as well give up forthwith all hope of further resistance. He communicated his views to the new Pope, Paul V., elected May 16th of this same year. The Holy Father at once entered into his estimate of the situation, and bade him start, without loss of time, as Envoy Extraordinary of the Holy See, to the Court of Spain. Philip III. and his Queen Margaret, whom Laurence had known in her maiden days at Ferrara, received him with extreme reverence and joy. Philip's active co-operation with the League was secured, and Laurence founded another Capuchin Monastery at Madrid. Hitherto, in Spain, the order had only three provinces, Catalonia, Valencia, and Arragon. The new house at Madrid, of which Cardinal Borgia, in presence of the King and Queen and Court, laid the foundation-stone in November, 1609, was the beginning of another province of Castile. Immediately after the ceremony he hastened to Prague. No sooner had he arrived, followed by reinforcements which Philip had promised, than a change of tone was visible in the princes of the Protestant League. Hitherto their insolence had been insufferable. Now they can stoop to send an embassy to Maximilian, proposing a peace, on condition of both sides laying down their arms. It was the happiest issue possible. The duke remarked: "All Germany, and all Christendom, owe a debt of never-dying gratitude to Father da Brindisi, for without him no League could have held together."

Circumstances were still precarious, and Laurence was appointed to the joint office of

Apostolic Nuncio and Spanish Ambassador to the Bavarian Court. The rescript from the Holy Father bade him leave Prague and go into residence at Munich (1610). In the following year (April, 1611), against the wishes and entreaties of Maximilian, and in defiance of all danger, he began a missionary journey through Bavaria, many of the imperial cities, and Saxony, then the centre and stronghold of the "Reformed" teachings. His zeal and charity were rewarded by a large harvest of souls and many wonderful signs of God's power and providence; and, on his return to Munich, he found all things in the good order in which he had left them, and his work at Maximilian's Court was evidently completed.

At the General Chapter of 1613 he is re-appointed Definitor General, and his thirst for rest left unsatisfied. Paul V. had welcomed him to Rome, in the spring, with every mark of affection, and had sent Maximilian word by letter of his delight at having the man of God in Rome again, after years of absence. His stay was doomed to be very short. The new

St. Laurence of Brindisi.

General, unable to visit in person the provinces of Northern Italy, sent Laurence as Visitor to the Province of Genoa. On his arrival at Pavia he summoned the Provincial Chapter. To his consternation their first act was to elect him Provincial. He protested on the score of the vastness of the Province, his weak health, and the paroxysms of pain that at times left him almost for dead; but they would not relent. He appealed to Rome; there came back answer that he must accept, and, it was added, that the Holy Father approved of the choice of the Province.

This meant another three years of toil and responsibility; among the rest, a fierce contest with the Duke of Savoy, who was also King of Sardinia, and was eager to separate the monks of his dominions from the Province of Genoa. The Pope had been won over by the Duke's reasonings, but would not decide without the consent of the Provincial. Laurence was unyielding in his opposition. He would at all times bind up that which was broken, and bring together that which was scattered;

he would be no party to disuniting what was united, and working together in charity and peace. So long as Laurence lived, they must evidently abandon their scheme of separating the Provinces.

His term of Provincialship ended, he visits on special missions Venice, Verona, Bassano, and Vicenza, and in 1618, the Pope entrusted him with some difficult negotiations between the Holy See and certain Italian princes. We may judge of the people's enthusiastic love towards one to whom the Church owed so much, by what took place this year at Milan. A common device of his for evading the people's "Here comes the Saint," as they saw him approach, was to dress himself in a mendicant's guise and wallet, and so pass unnoticed. This year no such device was practicable. They swarmed from town and village, far and near, till all the day long, for days together, the Capuchin Church, and the square in front of the Church, were crowded with thousands of excited people, gentle and simple, resolute on catching one glimpse of his noble face, and of receiving one blessing from his uplifted right hand. Distasteful as it was to his humility, there was nothing for it but, at intervals of every few hours, to mount the pulpit and pronounce his blessing over the multitudes that kept crowding in till they filled the church to suffocation. And as he left the city and they foresaw, as it seemed, that on this earth they would never look on his face again, the emotion of the vast gathering was literally indescribable. They wept and sobbed, and clamoured almost angrily for one more farewell blessing. What could he do but turn back and, mounted on the highest step in front of the church, draw from about his neck the cross which he always wore on his breast, and with it bless them as they knelt! The Archbishop, Cardinal Borromeo, brother and successor of St. Charles, had no idea of being robbed of such a blessing. "Bless the shepherd as well as his flock," he said, and fell upon his knees as humbly as the lowliest among his people.

The General Chapter, held on the 1st of June, 1618,—that same year St. Francis de

Sales had preached the Lent, at Grenoble, with results unusual even for him,—gave Laurence leave to pay a visit to his native Brindisi. A year more, and he would be sixty, but, except for a hurried visit as General, he had never seen Brindisi since his childhood. It was not only the natural yearning to see once more the spot which recalled the innocence, and the first joys and sorrows, of boyhood; but he owed Brindisi a visit as a graceful act of appreciation to his friend Maximilian of Bavaria. Maximilian, to show what he owed to our Saint, had founded in Brindisi, as being Laurence's birthplace, a convent of nuns. He had bought for the convent the very house in which Laurence was born.

On his way Laurence went down to Naples. To rest his shattered frame, as well as to escape the homage of Neapolitan crowds, he had gone to spend a few days at Caserta. He was recalled unexpectedly to Naples, by a message from the Cardinal Protector.

The story was soon told, by the deputation

of all the highest nobles in Naples, who waited on him with their petition. The Vice-King of Naples, vassal to the King of Spain, by his debaucheries (which had become a public scandal), and the taxation needed to furnish fuel for his profligate life, had reduced the Kingdom of Naples to the brink of open rebellion. Would Laurence—powerful in word and work—represent their grievance to Philip of Spain, for him to apply what remedy might seem best? The answer of the first moment was "No." And then he thought: "If a man shall see his brother in need, and shut up his bowels from him, how doth the charity of God dwell in *him?*" Then the Cardinal added his entreaties to the rest, and Laurence undertook to befriend them in their need.

So Brindisi was gone again—perhaps he knew gone beyond hope of being realized in this world. We have still extant the letter he wrote in his disappointment to Maximilian.

His first stage was Genoa, whence he took ship again. At the first Spanish port where they touched (Barcelona, probably), he learned that Philip and his Court had started for Portugal. He found the King at Belem, some four or five miles below Lisbon, at the mouth of the Tagus.

His journeyings were all but over. The rivalry among the courtiers, as to who had the best right to the privilege of offering him hospitality, was cut short by the King, who charged his confidential minister, Don Pedro, of Toledo, to provide him quarters in the royal palace.

We may pass over the audiences. After the fifth, it became evident that he had sickened with dysentery. The royal physicians were charged to exert themselves to their uttermost power to save a life so precious; and they were hopeful of success. The patient, promising unreserved obedience, told them that he was nearing the end, beyond reach of human skill. For five days, by an almost superhuman effort, he dragged himself from his bed, and said his Mass. He had never missed it yet; it was hard to give it up when eternity was so close. On the sixth day he tried, but failed. Perhaps it was the heaviest cross he had yet had to carry, in a life full of crosses; but it was God's will; and even now he could purify his soul by a humble confession, and give his Lord a home there, by the grace of a good Communion. This was his unfailing consolation, during the remaining days of his sickness.

After the feast of SS. Peter and Paul the Court removed to Lisbon, and the King—so as to have hourly news of the progress, as he hoped, of the patient—had him removed with all the care which the appliances of that day could secure, to a house adjoining the palace. Don Pedro was still privileged to be his host.

He had had one longing from the first— "not to live, but to die and to be with Christ." He had not much longer to wait.

On the 21st July—the Eve of St. Mary Magdalene's—he called his two religious to his bedside. He could not speak at first— they were sobbing so bitterly. He reminded them that, in a strange land though they were, God was beside them, and would lead them home. He was bound by vow to poverty, and had nothing to leave except this cross, which had accompanied him so faithfully all these years. Maximilian had given it him, and he had promised that at his death it should go, with the precious relics it held, to the convent at Brindisi. Would they see to it? And without needless delay find the General, and, on their knees before him, in his name beg his forgiveness for all that had been imperfect and disedifying in his religious life, and through him beg the prayers of the community?

Early next day—the 22nd, the Magdalene's Feast—he said, "*My* day has come at last— my day. The day of my birth—the day of my death." He made his last confession and his last communion; let us think of our own first communion, and reach up above that—oh, how immeasurably above it!—to a Saint's last communion.

Mid-day struck. Not till after mid-day did he receive the Last Anointing. Then, as the afternoon wore on, the whole family of Don Pedro, as though driven by an ungovernable impulse, came into the room to beseech the dying blessing of a saint. He was lying motionless—his eyes open and fixed steadily upwards—his hands slightly crossed upon his breast, but held between them the cross which he had no longer strength to lift. The bystanders just caught in a feeble breath the sacred names of Jesus and Mary frequently repeated. It was the only sound that broke the stillness that seemed more intense even than the stillness of death. He could not lift his crucifix, but with an effort he raised his right hand and blessed them as they knelt about his bedside. Then he joined his hands again, and kept them folded about his crucifix. And frequently, as before, there was a whisper: "Jesus, Mary," but the whisper grew feebler.

Three quiet sighs, and all was over. The soul was beyond the veil, standing in the Holy of Holies. It was about six in the evening of the 22nd of July, 1619.

There is no room here for his penances, his virtues, or his miracles. It has been difficult enough in a few pages to give an outline even of the mere outward circumstances of his life. From the first he had yearned for rest, but there was too much to be done. Labour without ceasing was the baptism with which he was to be baptized, and how was he straitened until it had been accomplished? Does he begrudge it now?

I RECKON THAT THE SUFFERINGS OF THIS TIME ARE NOT WORTHY TO BE COMPARED WITH THE GLORY TO COME, THAT SHALL BE REVEALED IN US.

ST. BENEDICT JOSEPH LABRE.

Not many wise according to the flesh, St. Paul was thinking, as he came away from cultured Athens; not many mighty, not many noble hath God called. But God hath chosen the foolish things of the world to confound the wise, and the weak things of the world to confound the mighty. It is a thought which constantly recurs as we follow B. Benedict's life.

Another thought we need to keep in sight is the thought which the Apostle emphasized in the letter which contains the last. It is this : that the natural man—we may call him the unspiritual man—perceives not the things that are of the Spirit of God, for they are foolishness unto him, and he cannot understand them.

Amettes (Pas de Calais), where Benedict

was born, in 1748, is not far from Boulogne—best known of all French towns, perhaps, to our countrymen. He was born on the day after the Annunciation, of pious Catholic parents, Jean Baptist Labre and Anne Barbara, whose maiden name had been Grandsir. John Baptist's brother was Curé at Erin, and our saint's mother was sister to the curé of Pesse, neither place being far from Amettes. One thing which characterized both parents was a horror of Jansenism, which at this time was dividing France into two hostile camps. The ull, *Unigenitus* (1713), of Clement XI. was still meeting with bitter opposition, and the bishops had been constrained to insist that their clergy, before administering the last sacraments, should require an acknowledgment of its acceptance. This had led to appeals to the civil tribunals; and fines and various penalties were dealt out broadcast upon such priests as had been loyal to the instructions of their bishops. From such an indication we may gather the state of religious feeling in France when Benedict was born. Add to this,

St. Benedict Joseph Labre. 59

that Voltaire, D'Alembert, Diderot, Rousseau, were all busy upon their work of destruction.

The parents of Benedict were untouched by the pestilence that filled the land. Their simple faith and humble lives were the most efficacious of safeguards, and an additional protective was the industry needed to provide for a large family of children—fifteen, when the youngest was born. The modest shop, however, which they kept, sufficed for their needs, indeed abundantly at the time when Benedict Joseph their first-born came. Their loving watchfulness was requited by him with an affection and a cheerful obedience that never gave them a moment's trouble. So again at school, till the surprise of the priest in charge prompted him to put his obedience and gentleness to the test. He blamed him one day for a fault he knew Benedict had not committed. With all a child's simplicity, the boy —about eight years old—said he had not been guilty. The master, telling him he was a liar, as well as guilty of the original charge, sent him out for punishment. Benedict made no

further protest, but went off at once, and
was preparing, without a word of complaint,
to receive his punishment, when a kind
word was given to him instead. A school
companion struck him one day severely. He
made no sign of pain or resentment, and when
the master, to whose knowledge it came, asked
who had done it, Benedict—perhaps over-ready
to excuse the motive—evaded the question by
pleading that the blow had been given inadvertently. Quick as he was in learning all
that he was taught, he showed, as might be
expected, still greater eagerness and interest
in the religious instructions that were given.
On such subjects he could never hear enough,
and on his return home his favourite spot was
the little room his parents had allowed him to
set aside for an oratory. He had built an
altar in it, and, assisted by his brother, would
go through the services of the Church with
immense delight. In the Church itself, to
which he lost no chance of going, he was full
of reverence and devotion, served Mass with a
quiet earnestness that struck all who saw it,

went frequently to confession, and followed with keen attention the ceremonies of the various devotions.

Pious as his parents were, they were somewhat disquieted at the eagerness he showed to break away from the world and serve God as a hermit. His mother was dissuading him one day, by the difficulty of obtaining sufficient food sometimes, in such a solitude. His answer was prompt:—the herb and roots that grew round about would suffice, as they sufficed for the hermits of old. But then, his mother retorted, men were stronger than they are now. "Yes, but mother," was his reply, "God's grace is as strong now as it was then, and if He worked miracles then, to provide food for His servants, why not now?" Meantime, he prepared himself for a penitential life by such austerities as sleeping on a table, or the bare floor, or with his head pillowed on a piece of wood; or, again, by leaving untouched a large part, or the daintiest part, of his food.

He was twelve when he left home for Erin, where his father's brother was curé. He was a man of most saintly life, and undertook in person the religious instruction of his nephew, sending him to a neighbouring school for his Latin and other studies. Here, as at home, Benedict made himself much beloved by his uncle and his schoolmaster, till, at the age of sixteen, he began to manifest an insurmountable dislike to his Latin studies, in which, so far, he had made considerable progress. Rebukes were useless—he could not succeed, try as he would. It was the road by which God was leading him to the future He had in store for him. All human science, he told his uncle at this time, had become hopelessly distasteful to him. There was only one science worth the name on which his mind and heart cared to rest. It was the science of the saints—learning how best to serve and find favour with God alone, and work out most securely his salvation. It seemed to him that La Trappe was the most rigorous monastery within reach, and the one therefore which he had better choose. His uncle was amazed; the worthy man had reckoned on seeing Benedict ordained, and having him as assistant-priest to lighten his priestly work towards the evening of his life. The evening, however, was to come sooner than he thought; in 1766, an epidemic visited Erin, and made great havoc among the people. Benedict was indefatigable in his efforts to relieve and console and minister to the sick and dying. He had never yet had such a field for his charity and forgetfulness of self. Before long, however, his uncle, whose own labours among his stricken flock were just as heroic, deemed it prudent to forbid his nephew to enter some few houses where the danger was exceptionally great. Meantime, as he lightened Benedict's work, he must labour himself all the harder. It ended as we might expect. He sickened and died, September, 1766. Greater love than this no man hath, that he should lay down his life for his friend. The good shepherd had lived among his sheep, and for them. It was granted him by one proof more to show what the love of the good shepherd is, by dying for his sheep, as he had lived for them.

In deep distress, Benedict returned home. He was now eighteen. This was 1766. The preceding year was remarkable by the decree of Clement XIII., approving the Feast of the Sacred Heart. At home he persisted in living a life of extreme rigour, and spoke constantly of his vocation to a monastic life in the house at La Trappe. Arrangements were made meantime for his going to live with his other uncle, the curé—his mother's brother. But his new life made no change in his mortifications, or his yearning for La Trappe.

He stayed with his uncle a few months, and then returned home. The uncle saw, especially after an interview Benedict had had with some fathers who were giving a mission in his neighbourhood, how useless it would be to put obstacles between Benedict and the one wish on which he had set his heart, and in that sense wrote to his sister. Finally, the parents gave their consent, and Benedict started for La Trappe. The distance was some sixty French leagues, the season extremely severe, the roads almost impassable,

Benedict's health at the moment precarious; but nothing could daunt him. He arrived, and—they rejected him! He was not strong enough; perhaps later, if his strength increased, they might admit him.

On getting back to Amettes it was hardly possible to recognise him. He was almost naked, and half dead with want of food, shelter and clothing, to say nothing of the hundreds of miles he had walked. He had no sooner recovered than he was for starting again. This time, perhaps, they might not think him so weak in health, and might receive him. His parents were aghast; to them it seemed little short of madness. They begged the second priest of Amettes to use his influence to dissuade him. His arguments were so far successful that Benedict, instead of going in person, agreed to write.

The abbot wrote in answer, that as their reasons for declining to receive him still held good, he must not think of coming.

La Trappe was closed to him; he would try the Chartreuse, which his parents had recommended when dissuading him from La Trappe. But after six weeks at the Chartreuse, near Montreville, the prior, satisfied that his vocation was not to Carthusianism, decided not to receive him. "It is the omnipotent hand of God which guides me," Benedict wrote to his parents in the account of his dismissal. He left Oct. 2, 1769.

Once more he stood at the gates of La Trappe. They would not swerve from their decision, and with a heavy heart Benedict turned away. By November 11 he had presented himself and been received as postulant at the Cistercian Monastery of Septfonds. God had another manner of life in store for him, which He chose to reveal to him, not suddenly and at once, but according to His wont, by slow degrees. At the end of six months and a half of inconceivable desolateness and pain of mind, Benedict was little more than a skeleton, and they had come to the conclusion that they must send him away. But they insisted first on his remaining two months longer in the hospital adjoining the convent, where his piety and gentleness won the hearts of all the Community.

Eight months' residence at Septfonds will bring us to July or August, 1770. On the last day of August he was in Piedmont, writing from thence the last letter his parents will receive from him.

That year, 1770, was to be a memorable year for him. It was the year when St. Paul of the Cross made the last visitation of his houses throughout the Patrimony of St. Peter, and on his return to Rome fell ill, and was very near to death. Farther south, in the diocese of St. Agatha, the Bishop, an old man within a month of seventy-five, finds himself able, on the 27th of this same month of August, to say Mass once more. It was the first time for two years, and the Bishop was St. Alphonsus. Four days after the Bishop's recovery, to his unspeakable joy, of the highest of all earthly privileges, another servant of God, in the first years of manhood, and in a strange land, is writing his last letter to parents whom he loved tenderly, telling them that he would return home no more, nor would they see him again till they saw him in the valley of Josaphat. On earth they never saw his face again. He did, before his death, revisit France, but never within a long distance of his home.

He was to have no home. That was to be precisely one essential part of his life. Homeless, that he might cast himself more utterly on the fatherhood of God; a beggar, even as for that matter we are all of us nothing better than beggars before God—the rich and the poor alike, as St. Augustine remarks, have to say, as day by day they stand before God: "Give us this day our daily bread;" heeding no more than if it had been dross all that the world worships most; so Benedict was to live henceforth. However else his life may affect different minds, it must teach them better that life is nothing more than a pilgrimage; that the man who loves father or mother more than Him is not worthy to be His disciple; and that on our Master's side, if He cares for the lilies of the field and the birds of the air, that toil not and spin not, so will He care for us, if we seek first His kingdom, and are anxious neither for food nor raiment. Are not ye of much more value than they?

From the time he wrote to his parents the letter we have mentioned, they never heard from him or of him for thirteen years. Then came news that a poor beggar man in Rome —" the poor man of the Forty Hours," as the Romans called him—had died a Saint's death, and was being venerated as a Saint in the Holy City, the centre of Christendom. There was proof enough to satisfy them that the beggar-man was no other than Benedict, their first-born.

As he journeyed along on foot, in that late summer of 1770, his mind became more and more filled with the certainty that what God willed for him was that, like another St. Alexis, he should leave country, parents, home, comfort, and all that the world values, and lead a new sort of life, the poorest and most penitential; not in a desert or cloister, but in the midst of the world, visiting, as a pilgrim the holy sanctuaries of Europe. By the first week of November he had reached Loreto. Then westward to Asisi, to kneel at the tomb of his favourite St. Francis (Nov. 18, 1770), and enrol himself as a wearer of his cord. Early in December he was asking charity before the gate of St. Louis, the French hospice in Rome. He stayed some months in Rome, but not beyond the spring of the following year (1771). In the Holy Week of 1771 he was again at his beloved sanctuary of Loreto. He left Loreto for Fabriano (some thirty miles westward), to pray there beside the tomb of St. Romuald, founder of the Camaldolese. Then down along the Adriatic to Bari, whither, in 1087, they brought the remains of St. Nicholas; and from Bari, across Italy to Naples, to offer his homage to St. Januarius, patronal saint of the city. Northwards next, into Tuscany—not to Asisi this time, but to Mont, Alverno, near Vallombrosa and Camaldoli, where St. Francis had received the Stigmata about two years before his death. Northwards again, into

Switzerland, to pray at Our Lady's famous shrine of Einsiedeln, near Lake Zurich. Then by Moulins, in the Bourbounais, where St. Jane Frances of Chantal died (1641), into Spain. To Einsiedeln he made as many as five different pilgrimages; to Loreto eleven, visiting it regularly year by year till the year preceding his death.

All this has a pleasant sound. We think of the heights of Loreto, with the Adriatic at our feet and villages dotted here and there over the plain, which is rich in corn and olive and vine. Or of Naples, with its sunny bay and burning mountain, and sunsets lighting up the islands in the offing. Or of Tuscany, with the purple light about the distant hills. We should have other things to think of, if we would try a week's pilgrimage on blessed Benedict's plan.

He had no money, nor asked for it; nor would accept it, when offered, beyond the smallest copper coin that would buy bread for that day's food. Bread was a luxury he would often do without. The cabbage stalks, or pea-shells, or orange-peel he found in the road often served for his day's meal. Or he found some decayed fruit, and was satisfied with that. He avoided the road or beaten path, and, still more scrupulously the villages and towns that lay on the journey. He slept where night overtook him, on the bare ground; perhaps, under a tree or the shelter of a rock. His clothes were rags, which he tried to hold together by small pieces of rope which he had knotted up and fastened about his waist. His shoes were almost useless; so full of holes that they were no protection against cold or mud or rain. His stockings were in tatters—he might just as well carry them, as he often did, in the rope fastened about his waist. People were welcome to hoot and pelt him; he remembered the silence of Jesus. "But Jesus held his peace." The vermin, that swarmed about him till they filled the holes of his rosary-beads, he made no attempt to remove. They added to his cross more than hunger and thirst and sleeplessness put together; he was quite content that his corruptible body, one day to be the food of worms, should be *their* food meantime. His neglected state should not annoy others more than he could help. He knelt in the least frequented corner of the church he could find, but if people would insist on taking him to their homes for food or lodging they must take him as he was. But many a time they found he had not touched the bed their charity had provided. And in this state he journeyed from shrine to shrine, telling his beads as he went along, on reciting, as he did every day, the Divine Office, or reading (another daily practice) a piece of the Latin text of the Imitation, or New Testament. Arrived at the place of pilgrimage he made his confession, and stayed kneeling in the church till the doors were closed at night. Then he would spend the night, if he could, just outside; sometimes resting his head on the little bundle, which on his journeys he carried tied to his back. In the morning, as soon as the doors were opened, he returned to the church, and frequently stayed there, day after day, without moving till night-time came, and the doors were closed again. At times, too, when he had satisfied himself, as he thought, in the great heat of the day, that he was alone, he would extend his arms, and in that position pray till footsteps warned him of the approach of others. Very exhausted, indeed, did he need to be before he would allow himself to stand for a few minutes, with the view of varying his position and gaining a short respite from the agony caused by two tumours which had formed upon his knees. They were each of the size of a small loaf, and with the vermin that tormented him must have made the pain of those long hours of prayer absolutely insupportable to anyone less heroic in his holiness. The day finished, he would perhaps dip the few crusts, which he carried in his pockets, in the water of the public fountain, and so make his one meal. He would rob himself even of his one meal if it were a day of fasting, or if other devotional reasons suggested it.

When, as sometimes happened, the piety of

the faithful, overcoming the natural repugnance to dirt and rags, constrained him to enter their houses for shelter against the inclement weather, their piety was blessed by the sight of such holiness as they had heard and read of, but had never seen till now. For one family who so received him, he wrote, with his own hand, a series of short Latin ejaculations and petitions, which he promised would, if devoutly recited, preserve them from the scourge of storm and earthquake. That was in June, 1771. On Easter Sunday, 1781, an earthquake, long remembered in Fabriano, where the incident occurred, destroyed much of the town, but the house where Benedict had been received stood unhurt. The little composition ran: "Jesus Christ, the King of Glory, came in peace. God was made man; the Word was made flesh. Christ was born of Mary, ever Virgin. Through their midst Christ went forth in peace. Christ was crucified; Christ hath died; Christ was buried. Christ hath risen again. Christ hath ascended into heaven.

Christ is conqueror: Christ is King; Christ is Emperor. From all thunder and lightning may Christ defend us. Jesus is with us. Pater. Ave. Gloria."

His terrible cross of homelessness and bodily pain was accepted by God in satisfaction for those other crosses of a desolate heart and darkened understanding, with which God often visits His servants. Only once, from the the time when, as a boy of twelve, in his uncle's house at Erin, he made his First Communion, and received Confirmation, at the hands of the Bishop of Boulogne, had the terrors and scruples of imperfect contrition had power to move him from his rule of frequent Confession and Communion. That had been at Septfonds at the age of twenty-one; and so fierce was it, that for six weeks he dared not even make his confession. From that time the trust that loves to show itself in nearness to our Master, in approaching to His Sacraments, had never been interrupted. Constantly he kept making general confessions of his whole life, and even then his confessor could not find sufficient matter for absolution—a fact which many deposed in the Processes. And this spotless innocence remained in spite of temptations of fearful violence. The Apostle had been tried and found faithful by means of the sting of the flesh, the Angel of Satan sent to buffet him. Our Saint must needs be tried in the same fiery crucible to strengthen him in humility, and to measure what his love of God was worth. For years the enemy haunted him in this same shape, but not once, even for one brief moment, did Benedict waver or prove faithless to the grace that was sufficient for him. For some few years before he died the temptation was removed.

Rome had become his head-quarters, so to say, from the beginning of his pilgrimage-life. His mode of life there was not materially different from his life at other shrines. He wandered from church to church, picking up by the way, from among the refuse flung from the windows, what would satisfy him for the food of the day. We often find him in the

Church of St. Ignatius, the Minerva, the Apostles, the Chiesa Nuova, the Ara Cœli, St. Anne in the Borgo, Santa Maria in the Via Lata, and others; but the first among his favourites was Santa Maria dei Monti, where the miraculous picture of the Madonna hung above the high altar. At night he would stay sometimes in a hole in the wall, not far from the Quirinal, sometimes in a nook of the Coliseum, sometimes in the Refuge for the Poor, conducted by the Abate Mancini.

In a short outline it is manifestly impossible to do justice to his devotion to the Blessed Sacrament, his fervent and child-like love of the Blessed Virgin, or the heroic degree of his manifold virtues. He had a particular devotion to St. Joseph, to the great Archangels St. Michael, St. Gabriel, St. Raphael, to St. James the Apostle, and to St. Francis of Asisi.

Signs were gathering which told that the end was not far off. His yearning for the visions of eternity grew more intense; his practice of prayer and charity and penance more marvellous in its heroism, and, as though the veil were lifting, he began to speak of seeing his charitable friends in Paradise if he saw them no more on earth. He visited Loreto, as usual, in 1782, but it was to be his last journey there. His strength was failing fast, and he had been two-and-twenty days on the road. The mountains were covered with snow, and Benedict was so benumbed and sore, that he sat down once and thought he must die in the snow. At last he reached Loreto, on the night of Holy Thursday, and spent the next day, Good Friday, in prayer, as usual, within the great Basilica, as though he had been through no sort of privation or fatigue. His hosts, the Sori family, with whom latterly he had accepted shelter, seeing that he was returning to Rome after an unusually short stay, begged for a few days longer. He would not stay nor promise to return. "If I do not come we shall see each other again in Paradise." It was the the last Eastertide he would see.

The beginning of the following Lent, 1783,

found him at the Refuge already mentioned, where, during the last few years of his life, he had habitually stayed throughout his visits to Rome. He was racked by a violent cough. Through the night, when all the rest were sleeping, the watchman could hear him repeating, "Miserere mei, miserere mei." Still more touching and more suggestive of the close tread of death, was the confusion of languages which another overheard: "O bon Dieu, O bon Dieu, Miserere mei!"

The good God was listening to his cry of pain. The director of the Refuge pressed the sick man, wasted by sleeplessness and fits of coughing, to go into the hospital. Benedict could not be persuaded. Then, at least, he begged him not to stay up for the community night-prayers; or if he would not accept so much as that, at all events to sit down, instead of kneeling, while prayers were being said. Benedict's keen dislike to the least remission of rule prevailed, and he was allowed to kneel with the rest. In the daytime he dragged himself out, with the help of a stick, to his much-loved churches—those more especially where Jesus was enthroned for the Forty Hours' Adoration. The "poor man of the Forty Hours" is getting near the end of his vocation. The Wednesday of the third week of Lent was his birthday, the 26th of March. Whether he remembered it we are not told; the aged parents in far off Amettes remembered it, we may be very sure. On the Friday of Passion Week, April 11, he made his confession. He had made his general confession to the same priest only last summer, and the confessor attested, after Benedict's death, that he had not been able to find, in that life so near its finish, matter enough for absolution. And yet in his confession Benedict had wept bitterly, as though he had been the chief of sinners; and he had gone at last to make his thanksgiving, his soul penetrated with the thought that he was another leper cleansed, whose duty was to return and pour out his gratitude to God.

On the Monday of Holy Week, the 14th of

April, he asked leave to communicate of Father Gabrini, who, not a year ago, had begged him to look about for another confessor. He made his Communion at the altar of St. Aloysius in the Church of St. Ignatius. Did he know that it was to be the last time he would welcome his Lord into the heart which had never lost its baptismal innocence? Before he left the church he heard a Mass of thanksgiving, and then dragged himself to the church he so dearly loved of Santa Maria dei Monti. He spent a long time there in prayer, and hearing Mass after Mass. On the afternoon of that same day he made a visit to the Church of the Holy Apostles, and it was noticed how utterly absorbed he was in God.

A great part of the next day, Tuesday, he spent in the Church of St. Praxedes, where the Blessed Sacrament was exposed for the Forty Hours. He had to stand towards the end of his visit, and even standing seemed a fatigue beyond his strength.

Wednesday was the 16th. He seemed hardly able to crawl out of his room. The warden of the Refuge begged him, time after time, not to go out, as there looked every likelihood of his falling down dead in the street. Benedict, as though impelled by a will higher than his own, could not stay; and with no escort or help beyond his stick, he tottered along to Santa Maria dei Monti. On the road he met the director of the Refuge, who kindly renewed his offer to find Benedict a bed in the hospital, and provide for his wants while there. Benedict was very grateful, but declined, and crawled on. It was as yet very early morning when he reached the church. With, if possible, more than his usual devotion, he prayed before the Tabernacle, and before the miraculous picture of Our Lady, then heard Mass, and remained kneeling a long time after. Two hours later than this, Zaccarelli, the butcher, who had always been kind to Benedict, noticed him, looking more like a skeleton than a living man, still kneeling. Zaccarelli, however, cannot wait; he has to go to his parish church in the neighbourhood, there to make his Easter Communion.

About nine o'clock, Zaccarelli was returning home by Santa Maria dei Monti. There was a crowd about the steps in front. What can it be? He went up to look. A beggar man had fallen down exhausted and fainting outside the church. It was Benedict. He had felt so ill in church as to be obliged to sit down, an altogether unusual indulgence for him. Then, as he felt a fainting fit coming on, he got up to leave the church, and sank down exhausted on the steps. Benedict recognized Zaccarelli's voice, opened his eyes, and nodded his willingness to be carried to Zaccarelli's house.

There he entreated to be laid on the bare ground, but they would not listen to it. He took off the outermost rag, which did duty for a cloak, and so let them stretch him on the bed and cover him up. About eleven the priest came, and Benedict, after answering his few questions, became unconscious and never rallied again. The physicians came in the afternoon. That soul was forcing its way through the prison bars, nor could they hold it back. The assistant-priest of the parish gave him extreme unction, while another recited aloud with the bystanders the Prayers of the Dying. A moment or two before eight in the evening they knelt and began to repeat the Litany of Loreto. They had reached the first title, *Sancta Maria, ora pro nobis,* when the clocks struck eight, the bells of Santa Maria Maggiore rang out, and—the quiet breathing of Benedict had ceased. Those eyes, closed since morning, had opened again to behold the King in His beauty, to see the land that is afar off.

That night the cry went through Rome: "The Saint is dead, the Saint is dead." It was the Wednesday of Holy Week, April 16, 1783.

We leave the scenes that followed on his death. Nothing like it had been witnessed in Rome since the May of 1595, when they buried St. Philip. Fittingly, as for a rising from death to life, and joyfully, as for a coronation, they buried him on Easter Sunday, before the altar he had loved so well.

The Teacher who had the words of eternal

life taught the glory of Lazarus and the disgrace and anguish of Dives. The Teacher that speaks still in His name, and with His authority, tells the world of another beggarman carried by angels into Abraham's bosom.

HE HATH PUT DOWN THE MIGHTY FROM THEIR SEAT, AND HATH EXALTED THE HUMBLE. HE HATH FILLED THE HUNGRY WITH GOOD THINGS.

ST. JOHN BAPTIST DE ROSSI.

Not far from Genoa are two little towns which have become noticeable for events which occurred in them during the last decade of the seventeenth century. One is Voltaggio, about fifteen miles north, then, as perhaps still, a favourite country residence of the wealthier citizens of Genoa. A little farther to the west, in the neighbouring diocese of Acqui, is Ovada. At Ovada, on the Epiphany of 1694, an infant of three days old received in baptism the name of Paul Francis. He will live to found the Order of the Passionists, and be known throughout the Church as St. Paul of the Cross. On Michaelmas Day, two years later (1696), in a church at Naples, there was another baptism. Of his eight baptismal names, the child will keep the first, Alphonso. He, also, will found a congregation, and become a Saint. Two years later again, Voltaggio was to have the honour of being the birthplace of a Saint.

His father's name was Carlo de Rossi—we may notice that De Rossi (written, however, most commonly *De' Rossi* by his biographers), was also the family name of St. Laurence of Brindisi. Carlo, who was sufficiently raised above poverty to be called *Signore* by his neighbours, was married to Francesca Anfossi. They were persons of remarkable piety, and especially remarkable was their anxiety to educate their children in the knowledge of their faith and in the fear of God.

Another child was born to them in the February (22nd) of 1798—John Baptist, our Saint. He was one of four children, two boys and two girls. The story of his childhood is the story of most of the Saints. Obedient to his parents, industrious at school, devout in every exercise of prayer, especially in the Church; gentle towards all who spoke to him, he could not avoid being observed and beloved in the little world of Voltaggio. Many of us must have noticed abroad, the schoolchildren seated at their desks and busy at their lessons before the clocks had struck seven. School life at Voltaggio must have begun quite as early. We read of the little schoolboy running off from school, at the end of his morning classes, to the parish church of Santa Maria, and being still in time to serve at Mass. Serving was a great favourite with John Baptist, and the sight of the prayerful boy moved many a villager to the sense of his own want of faith and fervour. The child's progress under his two priest-schoolmasters was most satisfactory; and his days at home were slipping peacefully by, when a worthy couple came to Voltaggio from Genoa for a few months of quiet and country air. They were struck at once by the young serving boy—who could fail to be?—and as they watched him more closely, his unaffected piety and winning manners so gained upon them, that they determined to secure him for their household at Genoa. They proposed to take him with them as their page boy; would Carlo, his father, consent? Carlo, satisfied that his child would be in the hands of a master and mistress as virtuous as they were gracious and noble, was disposed to say "yes" at once. But then his boy was only ten years of age, and his education, though advanced, very far from finished, and after all, a sound education was more for John Baptist than a home even in such a family. So Carlo declined. The Scorsas (so the visitors from Genoa were named) appreciating Carlo's fatherly anxiety on a matter of such grave importance, promised to send him to school, and interest themselves in his education as actively as his father would have done if the boy had remained at home. This set at rest Carlo's one anxiety, and the boy left home at the age of ten for the city of Genoa. And with its wealth and shipping and stately palaces, its busy commerce and its history, what a city it was to the simple folk of Voltaggio!

Genoa was not to be his home. One day two Capuchins called to see the Scorsas. They were on their way to Rome on business connected with their Order. "Giambattista," hearing where they were going, begged them to present an affectionate message to his uncle, Father Angelo, a Provincial of the Capuchins then making some stay in Rome. The manner and intelligence of the boy impressed them. They made inquiries of their host and hostess about him, and proceeded on their journey.

Besides Father Angelo, John Baptist had another relative in Rome—a cousin named Laurence, who was a Canon of Santa Maria in Cosmedin. A very glowing account must have been given to Father Angelo about his young nephew, and repeated by Father Angelo to Canon Laurence, for, one morning, Giambattista receives a letter from the Canon bidding him come at once to Rome. A hasty visit to his mother at Voltaggio, and John Baptist, then a boy of thirteen, starts for Rome.

Rome was to be his home, the scene henceforth of his labours in the sanctification of his own life, and in saving and sanctifying innumerable others. There will be nothing striking in his heroism, no wonderful powers of organizing and governing, no swaying the minds and destinies of kings and nations, no rapid and measureless journeying through country after country, no high position, no transcendent gifts, nor martyrdom. Nothing of all this. He was to be a simple secular priest in a busy city; looking very little beyond the sphere of his immediate ministry; working under the burden of enfeebled health, and of mental gifts left impaired or undeveloped by the shattering of his bodily strength. The dignity of his simple priesthood was higher than the vocation of the Baptist, his name-saint; he might surely be satisfied with that.

He was thirteen, as we have said, when he left Genoa for Rome. He began at once to attend the lower classes of the Collegio Romano. It is interesting to notice that

St. John Baptist de Rossi.

Rome, at the date of our saint's arrival, was profoundly excited over the controversy upon Quesnel's famous New Testament. Clement XI. had condemned the book about three years before this time, in the Brief *Universi*. Two years later, the Archbishop of Paris, Cardinal de Noailles, in a pastoral, had shown strong sympathy with the condemned book; and at this precise date a Congregation is busy upon a minute and patient examination of its tenets. Their labours will result in the selection of 101 propositions, to be condemned in the bull *Unigenitus* of Clement XI.

Meantime John Baptist is rising into notice as another St. Aloysius. There was not a young student in the Collegio Romano of more remarkable ability, and certainly not one more industrious and saintly. News came from Voltaggio of his only brother's death, and it was feared he might feel bound to return home to brighten his parents' declining years, and continue the family name. But he had already made his choice. He had chosen the better part, and it should not be taken from him. He studied as one who at that early age had thoroughly realized how largely the fruit of his priesthood might depend on the development to their utmost possible extent of his powers of thought, and on acquiring during these years a love of study. We cannot wonder that years afterwards his masters gave emphatic and unanimous testimony to the extraordinary progress he made in the manifold subjects of the Roman College course. But absorbed as he was in study, he did not forget the discipline which is more necessary and sacred even than the discipline of the intellect. The discipline of the will, the formation of character, involving incessant watchfulness, and self-restraint and government of the thoughts and senses. He knew that if he sowed sparingly in all this during his years of preparation, he would reap sparingly in the harvest of his priesthood. So, working, and watching, and praying, he passed through the earlier years of his course and reached philosophy. In Philosophy his success was no less remarkable; and at its termination he was chosen for the public defence, in which he gave proof of conspicuous powers for studies of this speculative kind, as he had done hitherto for less abstract subjects. At the age of eighteen he received the tonsure, and during the following year the minor orders, after obtaining from Cardinal Fieschi, then Archbishop of Genoa, the requisite dimissorial letters. As a help and encouragement to perseverance in his fervent life, he joined the congregation of the Roman College called "La Scaletta," and in his confraternity, as in his class, his fervour served as a stimulus to many of his companions. His joining the Scaletta was due to a worthy priest of St. Mary Major's, whose Mass at this time he was in the habit of serving, and with whom he was on terms of close friendship.

Naturally, a student of such promise was chosen for an exceptional theological course. He was told off for the lengthened course of scholastic theology. He had applied himself to the study which, among other difficulties, involved a severe amount of writing at the dictation of the lecturer, when the hopes of many interested in his theological career were broken. Nature had rebelled at last under his accumulated austerities; a seizure of the epileptic kind came on, and when it left him, he was little better than a wreck. His voice had gone almost altogether; what was left of it, startlingly unlike its old sonorousness, had become thin and shrill. Face and body had become pallid, the chest weak, and his head liable on the least exertion to headaches of frightful violence. Study became impossible, except in a strongly modified degree; the mere writing would have subjected him to the danger of another seizure. His food had to be of the lightest and scantiest. And we must not forget that this condition of things endured from this time throughout his life.

Others might have grieved over the distinction that had been snatched from him of a high place among the theologians of his day. It was not a matter that would have troubled our saint's peace of mind. What he had lost was the result of a practice of penance, undertaken out of the highest motive possible to us—a love of the cross of Jesus Christ. He was not one to begrudge any earthly boon lost in taking up the Cross and following his Lord. Some time earlier than this he had been reading an ascetical treatise by Segala, a Capuchin. Two ways of mortification were indicated in the treatise as especially worthy of being constantly practised. One was, the mortification of the tongue by as rigorous a silence as it was possible to observe consistently with charity. The other was, the mortification of the taste by never drinking—even water—if it could by any possibility be dispensed with. John Baptist had carried both practices to great lengths; so far had he carried the second, that he had accustomed himself to do without liquid food almost entirely.

When the course of scholastic theology had become impracticable, he looked elsewhere. A course of lectures, on the text of St. Thomas, was being given, at the Minerva, by Father Bordon, and was attracting at the time much notice, and very large numbers of students. The amount of writing necessary for following the course was comparatively light, and John Baptist joined the class. In spite of his broken health he became a prominent figure in the new course, and still continued such mortifications as prudence permitted. Cheerful and even vivacious as he was, he never relaxed in the custody of the eyes—so difficult, but priceless, a discipline in the streets of a crowded city. Many a time on the coldest winter day the passers-by would notice his hands blue with cold, but he could not be induced to wear gloves. Summer and winter he dressed alike, his outer garment, though made of the poorest stuff, being scrupulously whole and clean; nor, when he became Canon, would he alter what had been his life-long rule in the matter of dress. He would not tolerate from any companion the least word suggestive of any dangerous thought. By way of showing how full of mischief the least

St. John Baptist de Rossi.

occasion might be, he used to relate, with great shame, how, in passing a house one day, he had heard some indecent word spoken in a quarrel. And the word had haunted him and filled his mind with filthy thoughts for a long time afterwards.

He enjoyed no society but that of priests or students for the priesthood. And as secular society was distasteful to him, so were secular festivities. He went once, and only once, as far as we can learn, to anything of the kind. One carnival, there was to be among the other entertainments, the representation of a sacred piece. A young ecclesiastic, to whom John Baptist was particularly attached, was bent on going. That he might not go alone, and find himself alone in the midst, perhaps, of considerable danger, our Saint went with him. They chose the part of the building reserved for men, and Count Tenderini, the Saint's companion, affirmed on oath later that, as far as he had observed with close watching, the Saint never once lifted his eyes from the ground from first to last. Nor did he enjoy the crowds that thronged to the various churches on their patronal feasts. The sight-seeing element was too obtrusive not to cause pain to a mind like his. "We had better go," he used to say with a laugh, "to St. Peter's for the Feast of St. Mary Major, and to St. Mary Major's for the Feast of St. Peter."

In the February of 1721 he was twenty-three. A fortnight later he was ordained to the priesthood. It was the day after the Feast of St. Thomas Aquinas, March 8, 1721. He said his first Mass at the altar of St. Aloysius (not yet, however, canonized), in the Church of St. Ignatius. It was the church where his seizure had first attacked him some years before. Before the end of that month Pope Clement XI. went to his rest.

We can well understand his face being lighted up at Mass when we think how, with his earnestness, he would have laboured to make it in deed, and not in name merely, a means of sanctification. He prepared for it by fixing his first waking thoughts upon God and the

Spotless Victim he was about to offer in sacrifice to God. Then came an hour's meditation, made kneeling. Then half-an-hour's immediate preparation for the thrice-holy mystery. And, as the elevation approached, hands and body would tremble so visibly that often the whole predella shook. And yet, as one witness testified, there was something so far removed from the merely natural about the violent trembling of body and altar that the courage to question him failed.

The Divine Office was another aid to holiness. It was not a mere vocal prayer as he recited it; "he more resembled," says one biographer, "a seraph presenting a petition." Every smallest rubric had a sacredness in his eyes, and, as far as by most careful management it could be done, he kept to the canonical time for the several hours. He recited it kneeling throughout, unless he recited it as he loved to do, with a companion, or unless circumstances would have made kneeling singular. Later, when his life was almost inconceivably busy, he adopted the habit of saying Matins and Lauds overnight, but from the first he would never say his Mass till Matins and Lauds had been said. Putting off the recitation of Office—"as though Divine Office," he would say, "were a thing without interest"—was a form of tepidity he could not understand. No excuses or concessions, made on the subject of the Breviary by the less rigorous theologians, were ever accepted as a rule for himself in his own life.

"The way of a man in youth" is mentioned by the Holy Ghost beside "the way of a ship in the midst of the sea" (Prov. xxx. 19). Rome was eminently the city of the young, and the first shape our Saint's charity took was an active interest in the thousands (they must have numbered thousands) of students who, from every town of Italy and every country of Christendom, flocked to Rome as to the centre of Catholic tradition and truth. There was no resisting the Saint's earnestness and winning ways. Special services and sermons were organized for them, and on such days John Baptist might be seen hurrying hither and thither as the students poured out from their different class-rooms. He was the servant sent to gather in the invited to the banquet of his Master—only that somehow with him excuses were apt to be unavailing. His entreaties and pleasant importunities were sure to succeed, and it was reward enough for him to see the crowds that attended the devotions. Or, in the summer holidays, he might be seen, after dinner, with a huge escort of students, making for one of the large hospitals to soothe and relieve the sick and dying, and to wait on the convalescent at their meal. He knew that nothing would better counteract the dangers of student life than a love of ministering to the sick and dying. Students become so imperceptibly selfish and visionary—the dreaming of dreams and forgetfulness of others' needs must soon disappear in presence of such reality. And he knew what a guarantee it would prove to a zealous and efficient priesthood. The hour of hospital practice over, they would troop off to the Madonna dei Cerchi, where they would say the rosary aloud before her picture. Then away, as blithely as only students know how to be, for a game near St. Andrew's on the Cœlian, or about the Navicella. People took to calling him the Apostle of the Roman College.

Side by side with this went a very different charity. It was notorious that the herdsmen and drovers and cattle-dealers, who filled the Campo Vaccino twice a week, on market-days, were, as a class, utterly abandoned and uninstructed. What time had they, they would urge, for religious instruction and the sacraments, and such things? At dawn, before business had fairly begun, the young priest was about the Campo Vaccino with his pleasant greeting and kindly ways. As they stood alone, or in little groups, he would accost them; and there is no need to say, that almost before they knew it, his gracious words had glided into others no less gracious about God's goodness and the Sacraments which Jesus our good Lord had been at the trouble f making to help us. Perhaps they had heard nothing like it for years; perhaps never before. It had, at all events, coming from him, a newness about it, and an unction, and their hearts were touched. And there and then, when they were instructed in the few great truths necessary for salvation, and were stricken with grief at their forgetfulness of, or their rebellion against, so patient and good a God, he would lead them to a Confessor whom he had ready in one of the neighbouring churches. To give them courage, he would go with them as far as the Confessional, strengthening them on the road in their holy dispositions. And in that way many a saintly life was begun, and many were the poor outcasts who reverenced him as their father in God. He got to know them all by name —" And He calleth His own sheep by name "—and to recognise them in whatever part of the city he met them. He met one as he was crossing the piazza of St. Peter's one day. The poor fellow was coming from the church. The Confessor he wanted was absent; he would not make his confession to anybody else, and was going away unconfessed and in the saddest of spirits. The Saint exacted a solemn promise that he would be on the spot at a certain hour later in the day, and forthwith started on a hunt for the missing Confessor. It was nothing less than a hunt, but he hurried from place to place, following up one clue after another, nor rested till he had found him and brought him off just in time to St. Peter's. The countryman's face might well have brightened at the sight.

Hitherto he had preferred being free from the responsibilities of the office of Confessor, and neither had nor had asked for faculties. He went, after one of his violent attacks, a little way into the country, to stay a day or two with Monsignor Tenderini, Bishop of the place, and uncle to the young Count with whom he had gone to the sacred piece played at the Carnival. The Bishop had heard of Father de Rossi's works of charity, and recognised the great importance of every different detail. "But," he added, "the greatest work and charity of all you are not touching—the charity of hearing confessions." The result of the conversation was that the Saint applied for and obtained faculties for Confession.

Meantime Canon Laurence was breaking fast, and was most anxious that "Cousin Giambattista" should be appointed his co-adjutor in the canonry, so as to step into the benefice when he was gone. He was astounded at the Saint's opposition, but he did not know —how could he know?—that John Baptist, on his ordination day, had vowed never to ask for, and never to accept, a benefice. The good canon's favourite argument was that John Baptist must have some settled income to depend upon when he was dead. To a lover of poverty the answer was at hand: "God will provide, and if I have nothing else, the alms I get from day to day for my Mass will suffice for me." Finally, we are not told how —John Baptist's confessor must have practically decided the matter—the importunities of Canon Laurence prevailed, and John Baptist was chosen to assist him in his canonry. He entered upon his new office February 5, 1735, the year that St. Vincent of Paul was canonized. Our last date was March, 1721, the date of Clement XI.'s death. Since then Innocent XIII. had died, and Benedict XIII. had died, and Clement XII. had been reigning since 1730.

Two years afterwards (1737) the good cousin, who had been another father to John Baptist, died, leaving both canonry and his property, which was considerable, to our Saint. Within fifteen days, however, the new canon had got rid of a great part of the property, and, as if by way of proving to himself that neither dignity nor riches had power to alter his mode of life, he took as his lodging an old granary not far from the Capitol, so as to be within easier reach of his church, Santa Maria in Cosmedin. Besides assisting in choir he wished to take an active part in the parochial work. He began his work, and at once, from a desert, the church became thronged with devout worshippers. They appointed him chief sacristan, and the work of renovation began and was continued, at great expenditure, till the beauty of God's house had been restored. An ecclesiastic one day was betrayed into an act of levity as the procession went from sacristy to choir. John Baptist dismissed him on the spot before service began, nor relented in spite of appeals from brother canons, till very long afterwards, when the culprit had shown unmistakable signs of repentance. He began to hear confessions at Santa Maria in Cosmedin. His confessional was besieged from early morning, till it was obvious that his choir duties must be sacrificed or countless numbers of confessions left unheard. In his difficulty he talks things over with Monsignor Bottari, Provost of his Chapter, whose advice was: " Let the choir go, not the confessions." They applied to Clement XII. for the dispensation. He sent back a rescript granting the petition. From that moment his confessional reminds us of what we read in the life of St. Philip, or, within our own times, the life of the Curé of Ars ; only that John Baptist was surrounded

by none but the poorest and most ignorant.
The poor peasants from the Campagna came
to him in crowds—he knew how to speak to
them—and they were a class whose sins were
of weakness and of ignorance rather than of
malice. A peasant had accused himself of
having fallen into sin. The woman who had
been the occasion of danger had acted, and
was acting now, as laundress to his house.
He must remove himself from the occasion of
sin. The poor penitent pleaded that there
was no one else who could undertake his
laundry-work; that indeed she had at this
moment some work of his in hand. That
could not alter his duty of cutting off from
himself the occasion of sin. Some hours later
the Saint was disturbed in his confessional by
repeated cries of "*Ecco, Padre! Ecco il
fagotto!*" It was his penitent, who had taken
leave of the poor creature and reclaimed his
bundle; and there it lay, by the altar outside
the confessional.

Most considerate, too, he was in seeing that
they should not have too long to wait. When

there was a long interval before the next Mass, he would slip out of his Confessional from time to time and administer the Holy Communion to those who were prepared. Or, when the Holy Viaticum was carried to the sick, he would arrange that for the faithful who escorted it a Mass should be ready to begin the moment the procession returned to the Church.

The higher classes and the nobles he would not absolutely refuse to hear, but virtually it amounted to a refusal. His principle was, that the rich could find a thousand Confessors where the poor could not find one, and, therefore, if a *Signore* or a *Principessa* came he would hear them once, and beg that they would look elsewhere for a regular Confessor. When sickness kept him to his "granary," he had a small Confessional fixed beside his bed, so that his poor penitents might not be inconvenienced by his absence.

Sickness was becoming so frequent and aggravated that he was bound to leave the granary for healthier quarters. He fixed himself with the community of the Trinità de' Pellegrini, but he had lived nine years in his granary before he moved.

The Saints seem able to make the day of twenty-four hours suffice for work which other mortals could not crowd into thrice the time. We can only wonder and feel ashamed of our little efforts, as we read what John Baptist, with his shattered health, contrived to do. There were two works especially, besides what has occurred so far, for which he had a singular attraction. One has been referred to in connection with his labours among the students— his work among the hospitals. The patients looked for his coming with the eagerness we have most of us noticed in sick people. They entreated him so piteously to hear their Confessions, and to help them to prepare for a happy death, that faculties had to be obtained from the Pope empowering him to receive Confessions as a sort of Confessor-General to the hospitals of Rome. In one hospital alone, Santa Galla, "we stamped," says the Prior, "during the *Anno Santo*, or Jubilee Year of 1750, four thousand papers, certifying that patients had made their Jubilee Confession; and of those four thousand, Canon de Rossi must have heard the greater number." In all the devotional exercises which he gave or organized for them he was careful that nothing should be long. "Keep the sermons short," he would say to the preachers. " Remember that the poor creatures are tired, wasted by misery and infirmity, and cannot follow long devotions even if they would." Very solemn, again, were the services he held in the wards when an inmate died. He took care to be immediately informed, and in the evening, before the body was removed, he would pray with them for the deceased; and there, in the presence of death, he would add a few solemn words on the happiness of a holy life and the awfulness of falling into the hands of the living God. His connection with the hospitals brought to light a vast amount of vice existing in the poorest quarters of the city. Neither expense nor trouble was thought of in his exertions to set it right. He would write to distant dioceses, and draw up the necessary forms for the tribunals, and gladly undertake all the cost that needed to be incurred. But he would never allow the Confessional to become an instrument for begging. On no account would he allow himself to give an alms to a penitent however poor, nor under any pretext to receive a present from a penitent however rich. "Every present so received," he used to say, "is so much taken away from my power to speak out with perfect freedom and fearlessness." For his labours in the hospitals he felt himself only too bountifully rewarded by the love and prayers of the poor sufferers. He would not go to give a short mission in the neighbourhood of Rome without first taking leave of his poor flocks in the hospitals. Many of them he could not hope to see again. They would say a *Hail Mary* together, then followed a very short sermon, and after another *Hail Mary* they would all repeat his favourite prayer: "Mary, Mother of the poor, have pity on me." But even on earth God gave him a higher reward than the gratitude of the sick and dying—or was it, after all, only the answer to their prayers? He had no particle or shadow of the fear of death—" God has taken it utterly away," he said once, "in return, as He has shown me, for the little I have been able to do for the hospitals. Devote yourself to the same work of charity, and I have little doubt God will bless you with the like reward."

The prisons, too, knew him, perhaps, as well as the hospitals. Prisons of men, women, boys, he knew them all, and was never ceasing in his visits from one to the other. How could he slave as he did for such a worthless set? some one asked him. "To get rid," he answered, "of the hell inside them; and when I have got rid of that, and driven out the terrors and tortures of a guilty conscience, little do they heed pain of body. Patience to carry them through everything else is soon gained *then.*" The joy of one poor criminal, within a day or two of execution, found utterance in his emphatic declaration, that if the Pope came in person and begged him to put off the execution, he would not, if the choice rested with him, put it off. His work in the prisons did duty as a half grave half gay excuse for refusing the fine ladies of Rome who begged to be received as his penitents. What *would* people think and say of them if they could find no confessor to suit them but the confessor to convicts, murderers, &c.? They *must* really look elsewhere.

Costermongers, ostlers, butchers, and the other classes that are crowded about the *Strada dell' Orso* were a part of the community likewise that kept John Baptist busily occupied: so busily, that a stranger watching him, as he hastened from one miserable lodging to another, would have supposed he had no work to see to beyond attending to their spiritual needs. His illness drove him sometimes out of Rome, but the change was no great respite from his work. His Mass over, he would go into the Confessional and spend the morning there.

Benedict XIV., of glorious memory, had succeeded to Clement XII. in the August of 1740. He had renewed, by a special brief,

St. John Baptist de Rossi.

our Saint's exemption from choir, in favour of his laborious work as Confessor; and when, later, he determined to institute public catechism classes for the instruction of the criminals sentenced to shorter terms of imprisonment, his choice fell at once on the saintly Canon of Santa Maria in Cosmedin. So impressed was the Pontiff with the importance of the work, that he was quite ready, if a church could not be found, to reserve one of the great ante-chambers in his palace of the Vatican for the classes. It was work after the Canon's own heart, and for which he was exceptionally well fitted by his long experience. He won their hearts at once, and their attention then was easily secured. Immense results followed —indeed, how could it be otherwise? There was a visible reformation wrought by one who had as little thought of setting up for reformer as the simplest priest in Rome.

There was nothing of the reformer about him, and yet, as season after season came round, on the day before the great Ordinations at the Lateran, John Baptist would pray, beside the tomb of the Apostles, that those young candidates might be filled with priestly zeal and charity. Who can say what increase of grace in priestly hearts might not have been owing to his prayers? We shall know when the secrets of hearts are revealed.

The increase of his work as Confessor, from the catechism classes just mentioned, was incredible, but somehow he found time for it. And yet a fellow Canon succeeded in raising a violent persecution against him, on the score of his absence from choir. The Saint never showed a moment's bitterness or resentment. He took the only revenge a priest can afford to take. No brother could have been more devoted and affectionate, watching at his bedside day and night when the clamorous Canon lay dying.

His own turn was not far off. In the same round of labour the young priest had passed through middle life into old age. How he had borne up under the burden of delicate health, and almost superhuman work, was a mystery to all who knew him. But early in 1763 it was clear to the most casual observer that he had finished his work. The year before (1762) he had been persuaded to go to La Riccia, sixteen miles out of Rome, along the Appian Way— the Aricia of Horace's well-remembered journey to Brundusium. The Saint would have preferred Rocca di Papa, but others were against it and he yielded. He had returned in October to die, as he said, in his loved home at the Trinità. Through the remaining months of that year, and throughout 1763, suffering as he was, he continued to hear confessions in his room. What a golden opportunity it was for the devoted friends who throughout his busy life had succeeded in little more than catching a glimpse of him from time to time! Now they could hear his burning words, and ask his counsel and guide themselves, and read for him his favourite life of St. Philip, and promise him, as he begged with the tears standing in his eyes, to bring him news and interest themselves about his sick, and criminal, and outcast flock. Oh, how his thoughts ran on them day and night during those months of his imprisonment! Hospitals, prisons, penitentiaries, market-places filled with peasants, boatmen on the Ripetta—as far as this world went they seemed to be all his thought. A year or two earlier some prisoners were being marched through the streets, and had recognised him across the street and saluted him. His warm heart was all aglow with delight. "I would rather," he broke out, "have that recognition than be saluted by a Cardinal." And now his cross was to know that they needed his help, and to sit there and give no help—" strength without hands to smite."

On Holy Innocents' morning they found him unconscious, and for some days after consciousness returned, he was speechless. He tried to uncover his head as they brought him the Holy Viaticum, but alone he had not strength enough. He could just make the sign of the cross and hold his hands clasped. The end was not as yet.

The spring of 1764 wore on. He was waiting from day to day his Master's call, without a particle of fear, as he repeated to his Confessor: such was God's goodness for what he had tried to do for his *poverelli*. Earth had less than ever to give him. They judged it best to allow him to receive Holy Communion only on feast days. The month of May was passing. As the third week came he was praying and asking prayers that he might have strength to say Mass on the feast of his beloved St. Philip (May 26). He would ask them to carry him now and then to the little private chapel of the Trinità, to see whether he could stand at the altar. We ask God for a gift, and He withholds it to give us a higher. The joy of saying Mass on St. Philip's Day was set aside for the joy of being numbered with St. Philip and the Saints in glory everlasting.

On the evening of the 21st, his last attack seized him. A penitent came later; dismissing him, he asked his prayers that God would grant his petition for St. Philip's Day. Still later, two priests came; he was asking them about Santa Galla and another house opened only that year, when convulsions came on.

Towards morning he quieted. After that he did not speak; he lay still, his eyes open, like one waiting and watching. At nine the next morning he breathed his last (May 23rd, 1764). His Lord had come and found him watching, and before St. Philip's Day he was looking on St. Philip's face in the tabernacle not made with hands.

St. John Baptist de Rossi loved the poor. The world talks about them and writes about them, but the world would look a long time before it could point to one of its votaries living a life like this.

I WAS AN EYE TO THE BLIND AND A FOOT TO THE LAME. I WAS THE FATHER OF THE POOR. THE BLESSING OF HIM THAT WAS READY TO PERISH CAME UPON ME.

THE END.

www.ingramcontent.com/pod-product-compliance
Lightning Source LLC
Chambersburg PA
CBHW022139160426
43197CB00009B/1355